EILEEN PEERLESS POWER SKATING METHOD

THE ART OF TECHNIQUE APPLIED TO HOCKEY SKATING

EILEEN PEERLESS

iUniverse, Inc.
New York Bloomington

Eileen Peerless Power Skating Method
The Art of Technique Applied to Hockey Skating

iUniverse books may be ordered through booksellers or by contacting:

iUniverse
1663 Liberty Drive
Bloomington, IN 47403
www.iuniverse.com
1-800-Authors (1-800-288-4677)

ISBN: 978-1-4502-5113-6 (pbk)
ISBN: 978-1-4502-5115-0 (cloth)
ISBN: 978-1-4502-5114-3 (ebk)

Library of Congress Control Number: 2010911829

Printed in the United States of America

iUniverse rev. date: 8/26/10

Contents

Acknowledgement

Before this book had taken shape, the mother of one of my students, Jerene Maune (Thieman), an avid photographer, began taking pictures of some of my students. When I saw the results of her work and how good my students looked, I was amazed. I knew they were good skaters, but their skating abilities, as captured in Jerene's photos, convinced me that I had to get a book written to share my thoughts, ideas, and theories on the art of technique as it applies to skating and as it is demonstrated by my students. The students in the photographs in the book (and in the DVD) range in age from nine to eighteen.

Thanks to all my students who have worked with me over the years. A special thank you to Micah Dabao, Melvyn John Nichols, and Matt Ibarra, whose pictures comprise most of the examples in the book, and to Shawn Hart, the goalie. A thank you to the eight who took part in the making of the DVD: Melvyn John Nichols, Micah Dabao, Cole Simpson, Max Simpson, Sam Bentlin, and William Crane.

This effort would not have been possible without the parents of the skaters. The parents' belief in my method, their support of their children through each lesson, and their belief in the abilities of their children to be the best they can be are worthy of recognition. It is not always easy to attend lessons every week, month after month, year after year, but these parents did, and the results of their unwavering support is demonstrated in this book. I have been very fortunate to have had the loyalty and trust of the parents and skaters in all that I have done.

All the photos are of my students. The photographs with the skaters in full gear were taken by Josh Dubois, a New York-based freelance videographer and photographer. He also did all the filming and editing of the DVD.

All other photographs, with minor exceptions, were taken by Jerene. She gave of her time and enthusiasm to the project of photographing three of my students, Micah, (age eleven), Melvin John (age fourteen), and Matt (age sixteen), in action during a practice session. This book reflects not only her great photography but also her time and her cheerleading in getting me moving on this book.

I also want to thank Trina Taylor, site manager, and Carl Kirtley, rink director, of the Mt. Vernon Recreational Center in Alexandria, Virginia, where the video and photographs were made, and the Fairfax

County Park Authority: Barbara Nugent, division director, Park Services Division, and Judy Pederson, Public Information officer. I have had a long and pleasant association with the ice rink at the Mt. Vernon Recreational Center.

Introduction

This book represents my experience teaching skating to many hockey players of all ages and abilities. It presents my ideas on skating and the emphasis I place on the importance of the body to skating. The techniques outlined in this book are what I have used and have found to be most effective.

The techniques are based in large part on my own background in skills development. I have an undergraduate degree in pedagogy and a graduate degree in education. I have had the good fortune to learn skill building from some great teachers who knew the importance of technique to learning and mastering a skill. My background includes years of practicing and mastering technique at the highest levels. The one constant I have found is that the application of one skill can be applied to another.

For several years, I ran a hockey skating school where I used the techniques presented in this book. I place great importance on acquiring and building a solid skating foundation (technique). Technique building can take several years, but the reward to the skater is being able to play the game at its highest level.

My book includes three chapters: "Balance," which includes edge control and body placement; "Stride," both forward and backward; and "Agility."

Since edges are used in every single skating skill, the better the edges, the better the balance, the better the skating. Knowing where the body belongs in every skating maneuver is critical to improving both skating technique and balance.

A strong, powerful stride enables the skater to play the game at a higher level. An inadequate stride is a hindrance to speed. My students first learn the skill of striding, then learn it with power, and then with agility.

Agility includes quickness. Speed can come through power or quickness. Each has its place in a game situation and each should be mastered. In chapter one, I present one skill using power, and in chapter three, the same skill for agility and quickness.

Each skater learns differently from the next. While there may be one correct way to perform a skating skill, such as a forward or backward crossover, there are many ways, depending on the age and ability of the skater, to reach that skill.

Bad habits are easy to acquire but extremely difficult to correct. A bad habit may allow the skater to go fast when very young, but over time, because of that bad habit, the skater will get slower.

With the Peerless Power Skating Method, skaters learn practical techniques that can be used in real game situations. My hope is that this book will be a useful guide to those who want to learn how to get the most power from each skating skill, whether they are beginners or advanced skaters. I hope you enjoy using this book as much as I have enjoyed putting down on paper what I have learned in my teaching. My students have demonstrated their mastery and their success using the Peerless Power Skating Method, and I am proud of them and their demonstration of excellent skating skills.

I dedicate this book to my wonderful son, David, who got me interested in skating and who helped with the editing; and to my precious and delightful grandson, Adam, who may one day be able to learn from what is presented in this book.

Chapter One:
Balance

"Teach the body first and the feet will follow."

Balance is the foundation for skating: the better the balance, the better the skating. Balance means body. Knowing where the body belongs over the feet all of the time is essential. All skating technique needs the body to be properly balanced over the blades of the skates at all times.

The best drills for body placement over the blades are those using the blade edges. Mastery of the use of inside and outside edges is essential to become a complete skater. When you are performing edge drills, make sure the distance traveled on an edge is longer rather than shorter. The arc made by an edge on the ice should be no less than 180 degrees. This will help in getting the utmost in balance and body placement.

Getting acquainted with your Edges

Inside and outside edges are used in almost every skating maneuver. Edges result from a drop of the ankle either inward (for inside edges) or outward (for outside edges). Figure 1-1 shows both an inside and an outside edge. Figure 1-2 shows inside edges. The knee should not drop inward but should be bent forward to line up over the toe. The angle of the edge to the ice is 45 degrees.

1-1

1-2

Body Positioning

Properly positioning the upper body when doing edge drills helps with balance. To do edge drills properly, the upper body must be lined up over the gliding edge. The upper body does not stay stationary but rotates, depending on the edge. The upper body has a slight lean in the direction of travel in order to keep it lined up over the edge of the gliding skate. This lean keeps the upper torso balanced over the blade.

For example, the shoulders rotate to the *left* when you are on

a. a left forward outside edge (fig. 1-3);

b. a right forward inside edge;

c. a right backward outside edge;

d. a left backward inside edge.

1-3

The shoulders will rotate to the *right* when you are on

    a. a right forward outside edge;

    b. a left forward inside edge;

    c. a left backward outside edge;

    d. a right backward inside edge (fig. 1-4).

1-4

Free Foot

The position of the free foot (the one off the ice) is important because it helps the upper body achieve the proper position for ultimate balance over the blade edge.

Forward inside edges: the heel of the free foot forms an open *V* (the heels do not touch) with the gliding skate. This position points the knee outward, not forward.

Backward inside edges: the free foot is close to the gliding foot so the body can be properly balanced over the gliding inside edge. The knee of the free leg is forward.

For *backward and forward outside* edges, the free skate forms a 90-degree angle with the gliding skate (fig. 1-5). For outside edges, the knee of the free foot is lifted and forms a 90-degree angle to the gliding knee. The higher the lift of the knee of the free leg, the deeper the outside edge. Be sure to keep the knees at a 90-degree angle for outside edges. When on a backward outside edge, the bent knee of the free leg leads the body in the direction it will travel. On a left backward outside edge, the right knee of the free leg is bent and opening toward the right to keep the upper body balanced over the left outside edge. The back, rather than the chest, is parallel to the skate blade.

1-5

In all edge work, the free foot should not wander away from the gliding foot, nor should it be behind the gliding foot. These positions will cause the body to be off balance. *Always support the body.* If the body has no "home" or is not properly balanced over the skate blade, it cannot provide the balance and power needed for skating.

Arms

Arms should not be a factor in balance and should not be used as balancing tools. When doing edge drills, arms should be bent at the elbows to form a 45-degree angle between the lower arm and upper arm. The arms move with the body, not against it. So if you are on a left forward outside edge (fig. 1-6) and your body is turning inward, the right elbow should come slightly forward and the left elbow slightly back.

1-6

Edge Balance

To get a feel for inside and outside edges, stand on the ice with your skates directly under the hips, about eight to ten inches apart. Drop the left ankle outward to an outside edge. The blade will form a 45-degree angle with the ice. Balance the body over that edge by lifting the right foot off the ice. Cross the right foot over the left foot and place it on an inside edge, forming a 45-degree angle of the blade with the ice (fig.

1-7). Cross and uncross the right skate to get a feel for the balance on the left outside edge. Repeat the drill with a right outside edge and cross the left skate over the right to an inside edge.

1-7

Individual Edge Drills for Balance

1. One-foot glide, forward and backward (flats of blades)
Push and lift: Hold the stick in front with both hands at shoulder height. Give a slight inside edge push to the side with the right inside edge, bend the knee, and raise it to waist height. See how far you can glide on the left foot before repeating the drill with a push and a raise of the left knee. Keep the back straight and head up. Alternate pushing and lifting each leg down the ice (fig. 1-8).

1-8

2. One-foot glide, inside edge, forward

For a left inside edge, place the right blade on an inside edge behind the heel of the left skate. Bend the right knee and push the left skate forward, lifting the right skate off the ice as the left skate begins to glide. Drop the ankle of the left skate inward and turn the shoulders in the direction of travel (to the right). The chest should be positioned over the gliding inside edge. To complete the right leg push, extend the pushing leg to a complete extension (straight knee, fig. 1-9).

Return the pushing (right) skate to a *V* position with the knee bent and turned out slightly (fig. 1-10). The knee of the free leg does *not* face the same direction as the gliding knee. Repeat using a right push/ extension or stride push and a left inside edge.

Note: A bent knee to a full-length leg extension with a straight knee will be called a push/extend or a stride push (see chapter two). These two terms are used interchangeably.

1-9

1-10

3. One-foot glide, outside edge, forward

For a left outside edge, place the right blade on an inside edge behind the heel of the left skate. Stride push (push/extend) with the right inside edge. As the skate begins to glide, drop the left ankle outward and turn the shoulders in the direction of travel (to the left). The chest should be positioned over the outside edge of the gliding skate. The toe and the knee of the free leg will turn outward, forming a 90-degree angle with the gliding leg (fig. 1-11). Repeat using a left push/extension and a right outside edge.

1-11

4. One-foot glide, inside edge, backward

For a right inside backward edge, push/extend with the left inside edge, transfer all your weight to the right foot, turn the shoulders to the right, and rotate the hips to the right. (fig. 1-12). The right blade will follow the path of the shoulders and hips. Once you have traveled 180 degrees in the glide, push/extend with the right inside edge, transferring all your weight to the left foot and rotating the shoulders and hips to the left.

1-12

It is important that your body is always lined up over the blade of the gliding foot. Figure 1-12 shows the body with a slight lean over the gliding skate. The inside edge supports the body throughout the entire 180-degree path. The gliding skate does not push out and away from the body. Pushing out with the inside edge is a common error. This will cause the body to be off balance.

5. One-foot glide, outside edge, backward

For a right outside edge, push/extend the left blade and rotate the upper body to the left with the left knee raised and bent, forming a 90-degree angle with the gliding leg and skate. The body rotates in the direction of travel (to the left). The higher the lift of the free leg (fig. 1-13), the deeper the outside edge of the gliding foot will be. If your body is balanced, your back will be above the outside edge of the skate.

1-13

Note: When performing edge drills, the blades should be quiet. There is no need to make a scraping or scratching noise on the ice. If the blade makes such a noise, it means the body is not balanced properly over the gliding foot. If the body is properly aligned over the blade, you will hear only a crunching sound of the blade digging into the ice from the weight of the body.

Balance Drills: Edge Jumps

Jumps are good for balance and can be performed two ways: for power or for agility. (See chapter three for agility.)

For power edge jumps, start with a deep knee bend (fig. 1-14), followed by a hard thrust of both toes down into the ice and full leg extensions, or "knee locks" (fig. 1-15). When you are in the air, there is no bend in the knee. You must get as much power as possible from the toe thrust into the ice to get as high as possible without bending the knees. The ankle will be stretched downward so the toes are pointing toward the ice. When landing, the toes hit the ice first (fig. 1-16). Perform two feet jumps forward and backward.

Start
1-14

Take-off
1-15

Landing
1-16

1. Side to side edge jumps

Side to side edge jumps use a deep inside edge. Jumps are done with the body balanced over the front half of the blade. Place the entire body weight over the front half inside edge of the right foot. The free foot (left) will be lined up behind the right foot, and both knees should be deeply bent (fig. 1-17). Push off (or "throw") from this front half inside edge of the right skate, stretch the left leg out to the side in a full extension (locked knee) (fig. 1-18), and land on the left front inside edge with a deep knee bend. The heel of the blade should not touch down. If there is noise in the landing, the skate has hit the ice with the entire blade, the noise coming from a too shallow edge, or from landing on the flat of the blade with no edge. If the line of travel is down the ice, there will be a slight glide before the push off with the right inside edge back to the left skate. The jump is lateral, not upward. You must reach out and land as far as your leg can reach to the side.

This drill can be done in a stationary position as well as down ice. There is no glide in the stationary jumps.

1-17

1-18

Note: When doing edge jump drills, it is important that you maintain a deep edge and a very low knee bend; the deeper the knee bend, the deeper the inside edge in the landing.

To perform these drills properly, the front half of the inside edge must make contact with the ice at a 45-degree angle. This angle and edge placement are necessary to provide stability and power and for the body weight to be transferred from blade to blade. Landing on the flat of the blade will cause the skate to skid on the ice, as in a stopping slide, and you will sacrifice balance.

Repeat the same drill backward. Remember that you must always line up your body over the blade that is on the ice (fig. 1-19). Your free foot will be behind the skate and your body will lean slightly to the outside to properly balance over the blade. If your free foot wanders away from the skate that is on the ice or you lean your upper body inward, you will have no balance (or power).

1-19

1-20

2. Crossover edge jumps, forward

Start with a left outside edge, push with the front half of the blade of the outside edge into the ice, and jump to the right outside edge (fig. 1-21).

Alternate these cross-leg jumps forward. There will be a short glide of the landing foot before the next jump.

1-21

3. Crossover edge jumps, backward

Repeat the above drill jumping from outside edge to outside edge backward with the foot crossing *in back* of the skate that is on the ice (fig. 1-22).

1-22

Repeat the above drill jumping from outside edge to outside edge backward with the foot crossing *in front of* the skate that is on the ice. There will always be a slight glide after each jump.

Note: It cannot be emphasized enough that in all the above drills you must use only the front half of the blade and land on a 45-degree angle of the skate blade to the ice. The entire skate blade never lands on the ice. If the skate blade slides or skids on the ice, or you fall out of the landing position, that means the edge of the skate blade is not deep enough and the body is not properly balanced over the blade.

4. Crossover jumps, sideways (side to side)

To use the stepover drill as a power drill, balance your body over the skate that is one the ice and, covering as much distance to the side as possible, land on the ice with an inside edge. The front inside edge is used both for pushing in the take-off and for landing in the crossover.

The power comes from extending each leg (to a knee-lock position) from inside edge jump to inside edge jump. As the right leg crosses over the left, the inside edge of the left skate pulls under the body to "throw" the body sideways to land on the inside edge of the crossover (right) skate. It is important to balance over each landing edge, because the most power can be generated by taking off from an inside edge and landing on an inside edge.

To begin the drill, balance your entire body over the right inside edge and bend your right knee, keeping the left skate behind the right skate. Push hard into the ice with the front inside edge of the right skate, using the weight of your body. Stretch the left leg out to the side, covering as much ice as possible, and drop the front inside edge of the left skate onto the ice, landing with your body balanced totally over that inside edge.

To get a good inside edge grip on the ice, your right knee must be deeply bent and your body totally balanced over the inside edge of the pushing skate. Jumping from inside edge to inside edge is repeated across the ice, covering as much ice as possible in the sideways jumps, and always landing with a deep knee bend and with the body totally balanced over the landing skate.

This drill uses the bend/extend technique, which means that the pushing leg starts with a deep knee bend and fully extends in the push-off. Both legs are fully extended in the jump.

Additional Edge/Balance Drills

1. Heel/toe "cuts" in a circle

Balancing on one foot with your weight on the back half of the blade, make small, repeated heel cuts (like a comma or parenthesis) on the ice. Follow this with a short glide, with your toe gliding in the opposite direction of the heel cut. It is important to keep your body lined up over the skate at all times. Your upper body will have a slight lean to the *outside* of the blade path. If your body leans to the inside, it will not be balanced properly over the edge. Each time your heel cuts a comma on the ice, your knee will be bent. As you finish the comma and go into a glide, your knee will be straight.

This drill, which is performed in a circle, can be done both forward and backward. Going forward requires weight on the back half of an inside edge (heel area). Going backward requires weight on the front half of the inside edge (big toe). This drill will prepare you for one leg inside/outside edges (the S drill).

2. One leg inside/outside edges (the S drill, forward)

Push off to an inside edge with one foot, flip the blade over to an outside edge, and then flip back to an inside edge, alternating edges down the ice.

When your gliding skate is on an inside edge, the free knee (above the foot that is off the ice) is pointed outward; when the gliding skate is on an outside edge, the free knee is pointed across the front of the gliding leg. This allows the body to line -up with the gliding skate.

Note: Perform a knee bend and a knee extension of the gliding skate with every change of edge. The knee of the free leg forms a *V* as the edges change. As the skate makes the change from inside to outside edge, the knee of the free leg will drop down to form the bottom of the

V. This movement of the free leg helps the gliding leg bend/extend with each edge change.

3. One leg inside/outside edges (the S drill, forward jumps)

Repeat the above drill but jump from inside edge to outside edge, making sure your body is lined up directly over the skate.

4. One leg inside/outside edges (the S drill, Backward)

This drill is the same as the forward one-foot S drill except the foot of the free leg helps the body to balance and change edges. The free leg skate moves behind the gliding skate. The free leg knee remains stationary, but the foot of the free leg swings from side to side behind the gliding skate. If you are on a left skate blade, swing your foot from right (outside edge) to left (inside edge) behind the gliding skate.

5. One leg inside/outside edges (the S Drill, backward) Jumps

Repeat the above drill but jump from inside edge to outside edge, making sure the body is lined up directly over the skate.

Note: It is important to use the body in the above drills. Holding the body still will make doing the drills more difficult. Move the body as the edges go from inside to outside.

6. Step behinds, backward

This is an outside edge skill. When the left skate is stepping behind, the heel will be pointing right and the toe to the left (fig. 1-23). The toe never points forward. As the skate steps behind, your entire body weight is transferred to the outside edge of the step-behind foot. The foot in front gives a sideways push (with an outside edge) and comes off the ice ready to step behind the gliding foot (fig. 1-24). Your lower torso will rotate to the outside as the skate steps behind in order to balance the body over the outside edge.

1-23

1-24

As the outside edge is placed on the ice in the step behind, the knee of that leg will bend and the front foot will come off the ice at the same time the gliding knee is bent.

Note: As is always the case in edge drills, the placement of your body is crucial. Your body provides the balance. In the above drill, your shoulders and hips move in opposite directions so that your upper body can remain aligned over the blade.

7. Stepovers, backward

This is similar to the above drill except that the leg crosses in front using an outside edge, rather than behind (fig. 1-25). As one skate takes an outside edge, the other skate crosses in front of the gliding skate on an outside edge. As the gliding leg comes off the ice and prepares to cross in front, bend the knee, forming a 90-degree angle. Then lift the knee upward and out before bringing the skate down to take the ice on an outside edge. Your body leans to the outside of the gliding skate (and over the outside edge) as the free knee lifts (fig. 1-26). This body positioning allows for a deeper edge.

1-25   1-26

An alternate way to perform the above drill is to hold a hockey stick with two hands at shoulder height. Cross one leg over the other on an outside edge. As the gliding foot comes off the ice, the leg is straightened at the knee and the toe of the skate kicks up toward the end of the stick. Then bring your leg back across the gliding skate on an outside edge while the gliding skate gives a slight push and comes off the ice. That leg is then straightened at the knee to kick toward the opposite end of the stick before coming back to take the ice on an outside edge. This is repeated down ice. The kick is always done at an angle, never straight in front. This angle helps produce the proper gliding edge.

8. Heel to heel, 360 degrees

This is an inside edge drill that uses a 90-degree knee bend and deep inside edges. Push off with the left inside edge to a right inside edge.

While gliding on the right inside edge, bring your left heel toward the right heel (fig. 1-27) and glide in a circle on both right and left inside edges (fig. 1-28). The right skate is on a forward inside edge and the left skate is on a backward inside edge. The body is balanced over both skates.

1-27

1-28

Once the circle is completed, push off with the left inside edge and then immediately push with the right inside edge to go into a heel-to-heel glide in the other direction.

Alternate these 360-degree circles (figure eights) with two pushes in between. The first is to get out of the drill in one direction, and the second is to get into the drill going in the opposite direction.

As the pushing skate comes under the body, drop both the skate blade and the heel toward the ice. This will help keep the skates in an open position (heel to heel).

Team Drills

A variety of drills can be used for forward and backward inside and outside edges. Here are a few:

Start at the end of the blue line by the boards, facing the goal line. Skate to the outside of the circle (by the boards) and glide on a right forward inside edge around the bottom of the circle. Next, skate back to the blue line and glide on a left inside edge until facing the goal line. Then skate to the opposite circle, glide on a right inside edge around the bottom of the circle, and finish by skating to the blue line on the opposite side.

Repeat the other way using a left inside edge to a right inside edge.

Repeat using forward outside edges.

Repeat using backward inside edges.

Repeat using backward outside edges.

Variations of the above drills can include:

a. Using the two end circles, skate

- a figure eight pattern using alternating right and left edges;

- an oval going the same direction around the two end circles using the same edge;

- a figure eight with a jump to backward between the circles using a forward edge on one circle and a backward edge on the other circle.

b, Using blue line to blue line and both backward and forward edges

- inside edge at far blue line, turn at the red line, outside edge at other blue line;

- same edge at each blue line;

- figure eights using the inside edge at one blue line and the outside edge at the opposite blue line (this will use the same foot at each blue line).

c. Starting in the corner at the goal line, skate across the goal line using an inside edge at the far boards. Skate forward diagonally back across the ice to the blue line. Using the opposite inside edge at the blue line, skate diagonally forward to the red line. Switch to the opposite inside edge at the boards. Repeat at the next blue line, ending in the corner at the goal line.

Repeat the drill using outside edges.

Next, repeat the drill skating backward using both inside and outside edges.

Finally, repeat the drill but use a jump turn halfway across so that you begin with a forward inside edge at the end of the goal line, a turn backward halfway across the ice to the blue line, a back inside edge at the end of the blue line, and a turn forward halfway across. In this drill you will use the same edge: left inside forward, turn, left inside backward, down the ice. In repeating the drill back down the ice, use a right inside forward edge, a turn, and a right inside backward edge.

Edge drills with quick feet

These combination edge/quick feet drills help with a change of speed in movement. With one step over, the drill can be done down ice; with two or more step overs, the drill is done in a figure eight pattern. You must use a stride push going into every edge. The step overs are always followed by a stride push to get into the edge glide with power. The more step overs you perform, the quicker your feet.

This drill can be done using both forward and backward inside and outside edges. Begin with an inside forward edge. As you change from one inside edge to another, do so with a step over (or two or three), followed with a stride push. Repeat with a backward inside edge. When doing inside edges, your gliding foot is the crossover foot.

For outside edges, the gliding skate is the cross-under foot; the free foot crosses over.

Advanced edge drills

Using drills two through five in this chapter under "Edge Drills for Balance," complete a 360-degree turn before pushing off to the other foot. Only one foot can be on the ice during these edge drills. Take the time to glide on each edge as you make the 360-degree turn.

Right and left forward edges use one pivot. Right and left backward edges use two pivots, completing a circle within the circle. When pivoting from forward to backward, the heel is lifted off the ice. When pivoting from backward to forward, the toe is lifted off the ice.

1. Right forward inside/backward outside edges
Beginning with a right forward inside edge, rotate your upper body inward (to the left), lift the heel off the ice, and pivot on the toe to

a backward outside edge. Continue to rotate the upper body (now outward), glide on the outside edge until the body is facing forward, and then stride push to a left forward inside edge and repeat the rotation.

2. Right forward outside/backward inside edges

Beginning with a right forward outside edge, rotate your upper body outward (to the right), lift the heel off the ice, and pivot on the toe to a backward inside edge. Your upper body will now be rotated inward over the inside edge. Use a deep knee bend with your knees pointed outward in a *V* position. Stride push with a right inside edge to a left forward outside edge and repeat the rotation, with your upper body now rotating to the left.

3. Right backward outside edge (two 360-degree rotations)

Beginning with a right backward outside edge, rotate your upper body outward (to the left), lift the toe off the ice, and pivot on the heel to a forward inside edge. Continue to rotate the upper body to the left, lift the heel off the ice, and pivot on the toe to a backward outside edge. When back on the backward outside edge, push off with the inside edge to a left backward outside edge and repeat the double 360-degree rotation. *Remember to point the bent knee in the direction of travel when gliding on a backward outside edge.*

4. Right backward inside edge (two 360-degree rotations)

Beginning with a right backward inside edge, rotate your upper body outward (to the right), lift the toe off the ice, and pivot on the heel to a forward outside edge. Lift the heel off the ice and pivot on the toe to a backward inside edge. When back on the backward inside edge, stride push to a left backward inside edge and repeat the double 360-degree rotation.

Chapter Two:
Stride

"The longer the blade is on the ice, the slower the skater."

The stride is not an easy skill to master. Yet, it is simple in its execution. It includes three elements: a deep knee bend, a complete knee extension, and a direct return or recovery. In addition, the body must be lined up over the gliding skate and the bent knee at all times. A powerful stride uses the body for power.

The importance of a good, powerful stride cannot be overstated. It is the difference between an average player and a great player. A good stride involves the transfer of body weight from one gliding skate to the other, with the body always lined up, or balanced, over the gliding skate. This position is the body's "home." With the body lined up over the gliding foot, it provides the power for the knee and inside edge push against the ice to a complete extension. The body cannot remain stationary.

The way I teach the stride is further simplified in that the return of the extended leg is a straight line. The path the leg takes in the push out to the side is the same path it takes in the return. The returning skate does *not* touch the other skate in its return. Rather, the returning skate comes to a position just under and slightly to the outside of the hip. The push for the stride always begins with an inside edge and returns to an inside edge in preparation for the next push. (The backward stride is slightly different and will be explained later.)

There is no extraneous movement in an efficient stride. There should be no kicking back or any other movement to slow the stride. If the skate is pushed backward, behind the body, the body will be thrust forward and be off balance. If the skate returns to directly under the body or touches the gliding skate, the body will sway inward and be off balance. Power will be sacrificed in both instances.

I believe that good skating technique requires that the body be taught what to do, so the feet can follow. This is especially true in the stride. The body is the source of power. Without it, the skater expends a lot of energy and is still not able to go fast. The skater needs to *feel* what it is like to have the body fully balanced over the gliding leg. There should be a straight line from the head to the chest to the knee, and the toe of the gliding skate. Figure 2-1 illustrates the deep knee bend and the extended knee-lock position.

2-1

Forward Stride

Knee Bend

The knee is important in the stride because the stride push comes from the extension and lock of the knee. If there is a conscious toe push, or "toe flick," it may result in a backward slide of the blade on the ice or a kickback, resulting in a bent knee rather than a locked knee. When the pushing leg is extended to its fullest stretch position, the body will be lined up over the gliding foot, and there will be a 90-degree angle between the upper leg and the lower leg.

To begin the stride, drop your ankle inward so that the skate blade forms a 45-degree angle to the ice. The knee is bent at a 90-degree angle and lined up over the toe. Do not let the knee drop to inside the toe. With this 45-degree angle of the skate blade and the 90-degree knee bend, begin pushing outward (to the side) against the ice. Extend the pushing leg out to the side until the knee locks.

A knee-lock position is when the knee is pushed backward in the extension. The pushing leg is fully extended with the toe pointing outward, not down (fig. 2-2). The heel should be off the ice at the end of the extension. The body weight is transferred from the pushing skate to the gliding skate. The gliding skate carries the weight of the entire body, so it is important that the knee of the gliding skate is bent to support this weight. The chest is lined up over the knee, and the knee is thrust directly over the toe (fig. 2-3). The body *never* stays stationary while the leg pushes outward. Notice in Figure 2-3 that the chest is lined up over the gliding knee.

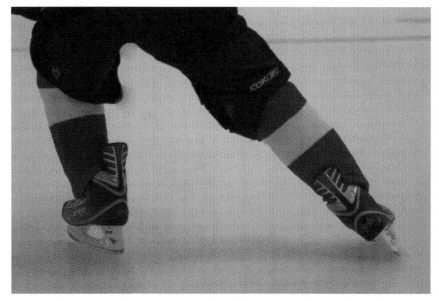

2-2

Note: In the stride, the gliding skate blade does not travel in a straight line down the ice. It travels at a slight outward angle (fig. 2-4). The two skates form a large, open *V*. The gliding skate never travels in a straight line going either forward or backward.

Knee Extension

The extension of the leg is not complete until the knee locks. That is the point when the leg is fully extended (fig. 2-3 and 2-4). The toe is also extended outward from the ankle. The heel will be raised off the ice. There should be a stretch of the ankle as the toe extends. In this stride, power comes from the deep knee bend to a full knee extension. The toe does not provide any power.

2-3

2-4

The knee is important in the stride because the push comes from the action of the knee bend to a full knee lock, not the push of the toe. If only a toe push is used, it is likely that the foot will slip back and behind the body, causing the body to be off balance. This will affect stride speed.

When the leg is extended to its fullest stretch position, the body should be lined up over the gliding foot, and the knee of the gliding foot will be at a 90-degree angle and will be directly over the toe of the skate. Both the knee and ankle of the pushing foot will lock in the extension of the stride push, and the toe will extend outward.

Return

Once you have pushed out and extended the pushing leg to its fullest locked knee position, the skate will return exactly as it pushed out–in a straight line to a position just outside the hip. There should be no kickback, kick up, toe drop, or any pattern made on the ice, such as a circle, by the foot on its way back to pushing position.

The importance of the pushing skate returning in exactly the same position as it did when pushing out cannot be emphasized enough. This straight line return will add to the speed of your stride. The knee does not point forward but remains in its position over the toe, which is at a slight outward angle (fig. 2-5). In the stride, there will be an open *V* position. In the return, the foot will automatically place itself on the ice in the position needed to begin the next inside edge push.

2-5

An important point in the return is that the skates never come together side by side directly under the middle of the body. The skates never touch. In the return, the toe maintains its outward angle, and the heel of the skate returns ahead of the toe. If the toe points straight down toward the ice, the knee will be incorrectly pointing forward. Figure 2-5 shows the proper knee position as the pushing leg returns under the body and as the skate takes the ice. Returning the skates too close together sacrifices power and speed and can cause an off-balance backward kick. In the return, the skate blade is never more than a half inch off the ice. Also keep in mind that as the pushing skate is returning the gliding skate is preparing to push (see fig. 2-6).

Remember that the push in the stride is to the side, not to the back. In the forward stride, the toes travel at a slight outward angle. In the return, the toes maintain this slight outward angle with the heel leading the return.

2-6

Speed comes from (a) bending the knee as far as possible over the gliding toe, (b) extending the pushing leg to knee-lock position, with the chest directly over the gliding knee and skate, and (c) returning the pushing skate in a straight line. If done correctly, there will be "snap" of the knee as it pushes outward. Remember that as the pushing leg is extending, the gliding leg is moving forward so that at the end of the push there is a diagonal line from pushing to gliding skate (fig. 2-7).

2-7

Arms

The most efficient use of the arms is to keep them under control. Do not use your arms for balance. Your body provides the balance, not your arms.

When you are striding down the ice, your gliding skate supports the body. To get the most power in the stride, the arms must move with the body. When you are gliding on your right skate, the right elbow swings back and slightly upward, and the left arm swings forward (fig. 2-8). With your left skate gliding, the left elbow swings back while the right arm swings forward (fig. 2-9). This allows the chest to be positioned directly over the knee of the gliding foot. Both arms should be bent at the elbow. These arm positions apply with or without a stick.

2-8

2-9

The arms will swing forward and backward from the shoulders. Do not drop the forearms downward from the elbow. The right arm swings forward with the forearm and hand extended, and the left elbow will swing backward with the forearm parallel to the body. The arm forms a 90-degree angle from shoulder to hand. The hands do not go farther back than the hip (fig. 2-9). To extend the arms all the way back expends too much energy and makes for an inefficient stride. This arm position keeps the arms in control, is more efficient, and less tiring.

The hard pull of the elbow backward helps with forward momentum. The movement is not unlike the use of the elbows when running uphill or cross-country skiing.

Skate Path

In the forward stride the toe of the gliding leg travels at a slight outward angle. It does not travel in a straight line down ice. The backward skate path is the reverse of the forward skate path. Whereas an open *V* is used in the forward stride, a reverse open *V* is skated in the backward stride.

Drill: Bend/Extend

1. Stationary

To ensure a proper return, stand with your feet under the hips about twelve inches apart, with toes pointing slightly outward in an open *V* position and both blades on an inside edge. Extend the right leg directly to the side; the toe keeps its outward position so that the foot is at an outward angle.

Line up your body over the left foot with the left knee directly over the left toe, which is also slightly outward. Fully extend your right leg and push the knee backward to the knee-lock position. Return the extended foot with the instep of the foot leading the return to the original position. This will help you get the feel of the open *V* position with the knee pointing at a slight outward angle. Repeat with the left leg.

2. Down ice, forward

When done on the ice, the right leg begins its extension from an inside edge that is dropped to the ice at the beginning of the push and then pushes against the ice directly to the side until the knee is in the knee-lock position. Once the knee-lock position is complete, the skate is returned quickly to its original position, an open *V*.

Because the toe travels at a slight outward angle and not straight down the ice, the knee will also be at an outward angle. This is true in the push outward and in the return. The knee never points forward. A knee pointing forward results in a toe drop. Always keep in mind the open *V* position.

3. Down ice, backward

The backward push is actually a slight forward angle. It is not to the side and definitely not to the back. When you are doing this drill backward, the complete extension puts the toe at a slightly forward angle from the body. If you imagine a clock, the right toe at its extension will be at two o'clock, and the left toe at its extension will be at ten o'clock. The toe is pointed outward and the heel is pointed inward as the skate returns to its position just outside the hip area. Only the toe of the extended leg will glide on the ice.

Once the toe is in position it stays there. The toe does not slide backward. It remains in its extended position until the other skate begins its outward push. The body is lined up over the bent knee, which is gliding backward at a slight outward angle. The gliding skate does not travel backward in a straight line.

Drill: Side toe drag

Repeat the above drill except in the return, the toe scrapes lightly on the ice in its return to original position. The skate pushes out to the side until only the toe is on the ice. The toe returns from the side to a position just outside the hip. As the skate is returning to its original position, the other skate begins its push out to the side, returning in the same manner. Do not hold the toe in its extended position but return it, on the ice, as soon as the knee has reached its locked position. The body transfers from one gliding skate to the other. Remember: the body *never* remains stationary. It must always be over the bent knee of the gliding skate.

Backward Stride

The elements of the backward stride are very similar to the forward stride except the feet maintain a wide stance throughout. A wide stance puts the skates at least shoulder-width apart. To get the fastest stride possible, keep the blade glide with each push in the extension to a minimum. The longer the skate blade is on the ice, the slower you'll skate. The fastest stride uses the shortest glide in the extension.

As in the forward stride, the body is always lined up over the gliding skate (fig. 2-10). The body should not stay in the center while the skate leg pushes outward. The chest is directly over the knee and the knee over the toe. In backward skating the push is forward, not backward. A push backward can put the body forward and ahead of the feet and, therefore, off balance.

2-10

Knee Bend

It is just as important in the backward stride as it is in the forward stride to maintain a deep knee bend in the gliding leg. When skating backward, you must make a conscious effort to push the knee of the gliding skate forward over the toe. Do not allow the knee of the gliding leg to drop inward. The push outward begins with a 90-degree inside edge angle. The body is lined up over the bent knee that will be pushing outward. The ankle drops inward to an inside edge and begins to push outward at a slight forward angle. As the leg pushes outward, the body weight transfers to the opposite leg. The pushing leg extends to the knee-lock position, and the knee of the gliding skate holding the weight of the body is bent. The chest is now lined up over the gliding skate and bent knee.

The push comes from the extension of the knee, not a push of the toe. In backward skating, as in forward skating, the feet form an open *V* position. The knees do not drop inward at any point. The pushing foot will return to its position to just outside the hip, or to hockey position, so that you can push out from each knee bend.

Knee Extension

The knee extension is exactly the same as in the forward stride. Drop the ankle to a 45-degree angle and begin pushing against the ice and slightly forward. The toe of the extended leg is pointed outward. As you extend the pushing leg, your body weight is transferred to the other leg, which is now the gliding leg. One leg is directly under the body with a deep knee bend; the other leg is extended outward and slightly forward, with only the toe of the blade gliding backward. (From this position it is very easy to go from a stride to a crossover and back to a stride.) This position is the stride push in backward skating.

The extended foot (pushing foot) does not slide backward and should never be pulled back in under the body for a two-foot glide. Having the feet too close together sacrifices speed and results in the body being off balance. There should be no circular motion on the ice. Remember, the longer your skate blade is on the ice, the slower you'll skate.

From the extended position, the knee of the extended leg bends in anticipation of receiving the weight of the body as the other leg begins its outward push. There will be a slight (short) backward glide of the skate that has just been extended before returning on its own to just outside the hip area in its "V" position.

Return

In backward skating the return is not to the center under the body. Instead, the skate blade returns to a position just outside the hip area, or under the shoulders. This provides the most balance when skating backward.

Once the extended leg begins its knee bend and the gliding leg begins its knee extension, the body transfers from the pushing leg to what will become the gliding leg. This motion will bring the skate of the extended leg back so that it can carry the weight of the body. The return of the skate blade will be at a slight inward angle (since the push was angled forward), with the heel leading.

Arms

In the backward stride, the arms—in fact, the entire upper body—remain quiet. The body and legs provide all the power. Moving the arms forward and backward in a backward stride uses too much energy.

Skate Path

In the backward stride the heel of the gliding leg travels backward at a slight outward angle (fig. 2-11 and 2-12). It does not travel in a straight line backward. The backward skate path is the reverse of the forward skate path. Whereas an open *V* is used in the forward stride, a reverse open *V* is skated in the backward stride.

2-11

2-12

Drills

In all the drills the following elements must be maintained:

- deep knee bend,

- complete leg extension with a locked knee and ankle, and

- a properly balanced body.

It is important to "feel" proper body placement. When you have proper body placement, you will be able to develop very fast, efficient forward and backward strides. If any of the above elements are missing, you can practice for a very long time and still not develop into a fast, efficient skater.

Do the drills repeatedly to get the feel of the extended leg with a locked knee and a stretched ankle. Drills start with an open V position. The skates should never be any closer than eight to ten inches between heels of the skates.

1. Body transfer, push and lift

Hold the stick in front with both hands at shoulder height. Give a slight inside edge push to the side with the right inside edge. Bend the knee and raise it to stick height. Glide for a short distance with the left leg straight and the right leg bent in front of the body. Repeat with the other leg. Alternate the leg push and lift. The body should be lined up over the gliding skate. (See fig. 1-8 in chapter one).

Repeat the drill backward. The push will be slightly to the front. Be sure not to push, slide, or kick backward.

2. Push and glide

Stand in an open *V* position. Bend the knees to a 90-degree angle, drop the right skate blade to a 45-degree angle, and push outward against the ice. The push should be hard enough to feel a "snap" of the knee to its knee-lock position (full extension). Return the extended leg to its position just outside the hip area for a two-foot glide. Do not bring the feet side by side. See how far down the ice you can get with just the one push. When the glide slows, repeat the push/extension with the other leg, always returning to the two-foot glide position. The push can be made at the goal line and each blue line; at the goal line and red line; and then from the goal line with a glide the entire length of the ice.

Repeat the drill, but this time push immediately with the other skate so you have both a right and left push/extension. The initial push should be followed with a quick recovery and a push/extension with the other leg, followed by a two-foot glide. This drill, can be done with three pushes, then four pushes.

The object of this drill is to see how much power you can generate from the bent knee and full extension of each push. The more power you generate, the more ice you cover in the glide.

3. Knee bend/push/extend, body transfer and knee lock
Stand with your feet directly under the shoulders. Bend the right knee over the right toe, and extend the left leg fully to the side. Drop the right skate to form an inside edge and begin pushing out to the side. Your body weight will shift to the left skate to glide. The right leg will be extended to the side in a locked knee position. Alternate this bend, push, extend with the body always lined up over the bent knee. Both skates will remain on the ice throughout this drill. Neither skate will be lifted off the ice. The extended skate will glide in its extended position on the front half of the inside edge. The heel should not be extended farther out than the toe.

Repeat the above drill backward. The extended leg is angled slightly forward, not backward. The toe will be at a slight forward angle, and only the toe will glide on the ice. The bent leg skate will also travel in a slight outward angle. The travel of each skate on the ice will be at an eight o'clock (left) and four o'clock (right) line of travel. Resist the temptation to lift the extended leg to bring it back under the body. The extended leg becomes the bent leg supporting the body. Your body will shift from side to side to stay balanced over whichever skate is gliding on the ice.

4. Push/extend/hold

Starting at one end of the rink, skate to the blue line. At the blue line, bend the right knee and extend the left leg to its full knee-lock extension. Hold this position from blue line to red line. At the red line, push with the inside edge of the right skate transferring the body weight over to the left skate. The knee will bend over the toe and the right leg will be extended to the side.

The toe and right leg will extend to the side. Hold the bend/extend position to the next blue line. Be sure the body weight transfer is side to side and not up and down.

Repeat the drill backward. Remember that when skating backward, the leg extension is at a slight forward angle with your toe pointed outward and your heel inward.

Chapter Three:
Agility

Agility Rule 1: The body must always be lined up over the skates.

Agility Rule 2: The skates (feet) must always support the body.

Agility is the ability to move in any direction: to stop, start, go from forward to backward, backward to forward, and, in general, to have quick feet to move around the ice. Maneuverability on the ice requires the utmost balance. To maintain this balance in agility drills, you must keep your skates under your body to always support the body. Neither skate should step outside the area created when you stand with your feet directly under your hips, about eight inches apart. In every agility maneuver, the feet must support the body. If a skate travels outside this "body zone," imbalance and an inability to perform the drill properly will result.

Remember, you skate with your body, not your feet. Skaters who are able to use their bodies are better skaters than those who concentrate only on what their feet are doing. This is especially true in agility drills.

The following are examples and explanations of agility skills.

Stops

A hockey stop uses both an inside and an outside edge with skates parallel. Both feet will be under and supporting the body. The blades form a 45-degree angle to the ice. When you are learning the hockey stop, keep your shoulders and chest facing the line of travel. When you stop, turn your lower body in the direction of the stop with your feet following. Thus, if the toes point to the left, the hips turn to the left so that your stomach is over the toes and facing the same direction as the toes. Your shoulders do not turn but remain facing front. This body position helps create traction of the blades on the ice for a better stop. Always begin the stop by turning your hips first, followed by your feet. The skates remain parallel and about twelve to fifteen inches apart. If the feet come too close together, or if the feet are too far apart, the body will be off balance.

The following drills will help to achieve the use of edges in the stop.

Inside edge stop

With an inside edge of the right skate, push the body forward, pick up your right skate, and turn your right toe inward. Next, place the right inside edge on the ice with the toe pointing inward and begin scraping the inside edge on the ice to stop (fig. 3-1). The right toe is turned inward at a 90-degree angle to the left skate and scrapes the ice in a forward motion to stop. Now turn your hips in the direction of the right toe so that your stomach is facing in the same direction as the right toe. Do not turn your shoulders. Your right hip will be facing the line of travel and will be directly under your chest, which faces forward.

Repeat with other foot. Push forward with the inside edge of the left skate to give you a forward impetus, and repeat the stop with the left toe inward, scraping the inside edge forward on the ice to a stop.

3-1

Outside edge stop

With an inside edge of the left skate, push the body forward. Now pick up the left skate and place it behind the right gliding skate to form an inverted *T*, pointing the toe of the left skate outward. Drop the ankle backward toward the ice so the scrape on the ice is with the outside edge of the left skate. When you are practicing this stop, keep your shoulders forward; do not turn them. Repeat with the right outside edge.

A helpful aid in mastering this stop is to hold the right arm forward when stopping on a right outside edge and the left arm forward when stopping on a left outside edge. This keeps the body in a balanced position. Be sure to bend the knees in the stop.

Figure 3-2 demonstrates an outside edge stop.

3-2

Two-foot stop

Hold your arms at shoulder level in front of your body. This ensures proper balance when practicing the two-foot stop. Push yourself forward with an inside edge of one skate, do a two-foot glide with your feet about ten to twelve inches apart (fig. 3-4), and rotate your hips to either the right or left (depending on which way you wish to stop). Your arms and shoulders will remain in the same position; only your lower body will turn. This position is similar to a stop in skiing.

The feet follow the lower body in the turn, not the other way round (fig. 3-3). Both edges scrape the ice in the stop, not just the inside edge of the front foot. Repetition will help to feel the turn of the lower body.

3-3

3-4

To keep your shoulders and hips moving separately from one another, a helpful aid is to swing your arms in the opposite direction of your hips or stomach. This gives added balance in the stop and helps you feel the rotation.

Practice drills

1. Outside edge stop

Stand on the blue line. With the entire right skate on the blue line and the toe pointing toward the board, place the left skate in the *T* position. Pushing with the left inside edge, glide on the right blade that is on the blue line. Pick up the left skate after the push, drop the ankle backward so that the outside edge scrapes the ice behind the heel of the right skate, and come to a stop on the left outside edge. The position, or pressure on the blade in the stop, is where your little toe is in the skate boot.

Balance your weight on the outside edge, pick up the right skate, cross it over the left skate, and begin an inside edge push in the opposite direction. The left skate will be entirely on the blue line. Repeat the outside edge stop with the right skate.

Alternately, the above drill can be done side to side on a straight line, or down the ice in a *V* position so that the skate travels at an angle, first to the left and then to the right.

The drill also can be done using only the outside edge for the stop, with the front skate lifted off the ice. The front skate will leave the ice as soon as the back skate touches down for the scrape, or stop. The lifted skate then crosses over the stopping skate to repeat the drill to the other side. Always remember to push with the inside edge after it crosses over the stopping skate.

2. Side-to-side hockey stops

When you are doing side-to-side hockey stops, do not lift the back foot off the ice in the turn to stop. Both skates glide into the turn to stop because both skates are needed to support the body. The placement of the skates in the stop should be narrower than the width of the shoulders. Practice the two-foot, or hockey stop, with three strides and a stop, then two strides and a stop, and then one stride and a stop. The ability to go from right to left stops with only one push requires agility. Turn your hips with the feet (fig. 3-6 and 3-8) and keep your upper body forward.

Another drill to practice hockey stops is to take three stepovers to the right and stop, followed by three stepovers to the left and stop. In this drill the entire body faces forward. There is no turning of the hips. The upper body has a slight outward lean in order for it to be balanced over the skates (fig. 3-5 and 3-7).

This drill can be done with two stepovers and then one stepover. It also can be done both forward and backward, but always with a hockey stop.

3-5

3-6

3-7

3-8

Rotation Turns

Rotations turns go from forward to backward or backward to forward always in the same direction. All turns are agility maneuvers. In all turns the upper body and the lower body each have important roles to play. Understanding how the body functions in both rotation turns and power turns makes mastering them easier.

Forward to backward turns down ice

There are two ways to turn from forward to backward when continuing in the same direction. One is to turn going straight down ice; the other is to turn on an arc or half circle. These latter turns are useful in zone play.

When you are turning, the weight of your body transfers from the lead skate, which faces forward, to the other skate, which faces the opposite direction. Both skates leave the ice briefly as the turn is made. The weight of the body is transferred from the front (lead) skate to the back skate (which is gliding backward) once the turn is made. It is important to place your body squarely over the gliding skate. If your body is not properly placed, you will lose balance. In the turn, your stomach rotates from directly over the front skate to directly over the backward gliding skate. Rotating the lower body180-degrees, makes the turn possible. The body balances over the front skate gliding forward and then rotates 180 degrees to balance over the left (backward gliding) skate. When you are turning from backward to forward, the rotation of the body is the same. The body is balanced entirely on the backward gliding skate and then rotates 180 degrees to face the other skate, which is now gliding forward. Remember: *all turns are done with the body, not the feet.* Concentrate on body movement, not feet movement.

When you are turning from forward to backward or backward to forward, always bend the knee over the pushing skate. From this bent-knee position, the back foot is off the ice, the stomach is rotated 180 degrees, and the skate that is off the ice lands on the ice gliding backward (or forward depending on the turn). When you are turning, be sure the toe does not point to the side. The skates must form an exact

180-degree angle. If the skate does not land at the correct angle, your balance is off and you may fall.

The better you can do a one-foot glide, both forward and backward, the better the turn. In making the turn, there is always a one-foot glide forward or backward, depending on the direction of the turn, and a push down into the ice to facilitate the jump of the 180-degree turn.

Drills for rotation turns

1. Stationary turn: two-foot turn/jump

Stand facing in one direction. Hold a stick in two hands on the left side of the body. The stick will be parallel with your left hip. Bend both knees, push off with the front half of both blades, and jump 180 degrees in the direction of the stick to face in the opposite direction. The stick will now be parallel to the right hip. Do *not* rotate your shoulders. The shoulders and stick remain in the same position throughout the drill. If the shoulders are used in the turn, the body will over-rotate and be off balance.

Repeat these 180-degree jumps to get the feel of the lower body rotation. Remember that the arms remain stationery. The turn is done with a two-foot jump and a 180-degree rotation of the hips. Only the hips move.

2. Stationary turn: one-foot turn/jump

Repeat the above drill, but instead of pushing off on two skates and landing on two skates, push off on one skate and land on the other skate. Each skate's toe will be pointing in opposite directions. Always jump in the direction of the raised skate.

3. Moving turn: one-foot turn/jump forward to backward, backward to forward

Push off with a right inside edge and place the entire weight of the body over the left skate. (This push gives momentum to move on the ice.) Your body must be balanced over the gliding skate at all times. Bend the knee, push the toe of the gliding skate down into the ice, and jump 180 degrees to face the opposite direction, rotating the stomach so that it is directly over the landing skate. The rotation of the stomach is the same as in the stationary turn, but now the skates are gliding on the ice. The toe of the gliding skate should always be straight, not angled. You can hold a stick to the side, as in the stationary turn, to make sure you do not rotate your shoulders.

Once the turn is made, both skates can take the ice or another rotation turn can be made back in the other direction. This technique is the same whether turning forward to backward or backward to forward.

4. Moving turn: edge to edge

Repeat the above drill, this time pushing harder into the ice to get movement. Push off from the right skate to the left skate, back to the right skate, and then back to the left skate (fig. 3-9). This drill will help get the feel of the rotation of the lower body while the upper body remains static. Over-rotation of the stomach will help ensure that you make a complete 180-degree rotation.

3-9

Things to Remember When Doing Turns

In the forward to backward turn skates do not touch when making the turn. Once the turn is made to backward, the skates remain outside the hip area in the backward glide. This provides for the best body balance. If the skates are too close, balance is sacrificed.

When turning from backward to forward, the turning skate must not reach forward to take the ice; it must remain under the body to maintain balance. The skate gliding backward pushes as the turn is made from backward to forward. A way to make sure the feet are under the body in the turn from backward to forward is to tap the backward gliding skate's heel before taking the ice.

Neither the head nor the shoulders are used to turn. Only a 180-degree rotation of the stomach makes the turn.

Heel-to-Heel Edge Turns

This turn is similar to the 360-degree turn in chapter one. The weight of the body will transfer alternately from one inside edge to the other when making this turn.

Push off with the left inside edge to a right inside edge. Your body will be positioned directly over the gliding skate. While you are gliding on the right inside edge, bring the left heel toward the right heel, rotate the hips so that the stomach faces the toe of the gliding skate, and place the left inside edge on the ice. Your body weight is now transferred to the left skate.

Once the left backward inside edge takes the ice, the right skate comes off the ice and is placed shoulder-width apart from the backward gliding skate. At this point your body weight goes from the left gliding skate to the right skate, which is now gliding backward. Bend/extend the right knee, transferring the body weight back to the left inside edge. Once your body weight has transferred back to the left gliding skate, the right skate comes off the ice and turns forward. Once the right skate has taken the ice with a forward inside edge, the left skate comes off the ice and is placed beside the forward gliding skate shoulder-width apart. The body weight then transfers to the left skate as it prepares to push to a right forward inside edge and a left backward inside edge to repeat the turn.

Do not step, jump, or hop when performing this drill. All the transfers of weight should be done smoothly from one edge to the other.

Drills for edge turns

1. Inside forward to inside backward to inside forward

This drill is done on a circle. Glide forward on a right inside edge with the body balanced over the skate. Bring the left skate down, with the heels of both skates facing one another. The left skate will be on a backward inside edge. Rotate your body to backward as the right skate comes off the ice. Once the turn is made, your body will be balanced over the left skate. Pick up the right skate and place it parallel to the left skate, about fifteen inches apart. Transfer the body weight to the right skate while gliding backward. Give a push with the right inside edge, transferring the body weight back to the inside edge of the left skate. Pick up the right skate, turn it forward, and place it on an inside edge forward. Push with the left inside edge, pick up the skate, and place it parallel to the right skate, about fifteen inches apart.

Repeat the drill going from forward to backward and backward to forward with inside edges. Always transfer the weight from one skate to the other when making the turn.

2. Using the two end circles of the rink

Start in a corner by the goal line. Skate to the top of the circle, perform the edge turn forward to backward, and then backward to forward. Skate forward to the bottom of the next circle and repeat the turn, beginning with the left inside edge forward to a right inside edge backward. Turn forward and skate to the blue line. Do not jump the turns. Repeat back.

3. Using the four face-off dots between the blue lines of the rink

This drill can be done using the four center face-off dots inside the blue lines. Do all the turns in the same direction at each of the four dots before reversing to the other direction. When making the turns forward and backward, the chest will always face the dots.

Start at one of the face-off dots. Skate to the next face-off dot, push with the inside edge of the left skate blade, and transfer your body weight to the right inside edge. Next, transfer your body weight from the front skate to the back left inside edge turning backward, place the right skate on the ice parallel to the left, transfer your body weight to the right skate, push off with the right inside edge, and turn forward.

Your body weight will be on the left skate gliding backward. Push with the left inside edge, turning to place the body weight on the right inside edge to face forward.

The turns should be done smoothly from one edge to another, with no strides or jumps between the turns.

Repeat the drill at each faceoff dot. Reverse the direction so that the left inside edge leads in the turn.

Power Turns

Power turns come from one direction and go back in the same direction. They are known by a variety of names, including "tight turn" and edge turn. These turns become a tight turn at speed if two elements are present—deep edges and upper body placement. Balance is crucial in this turn to keep from falling and to keep the back skate from sliding out.

The weight of your body should be directly over the back half of the blades and balanced on the inside edge of the back foot. If your weight is too far forward, the back foot can slip at higher speeds because it does not have enough weight to keep the edge secured on the ice.

3-10

The inside edge of the back foot keeps the body stable on the ice. The front foot is on an outside edge at a 45-degree angle (fig. 3-10). In order to get the proper edge, drop the ankle of the front skate to the outside as far as it will go. (Make sure your laces are not tied so tight that your ankle cannot flex.) This skate position will help you get a good outside edge when turning. A common mistake is to have the front skate on the flat of the blade. If the outside edge is not deep enough, it is difficult to make a proper turn.

Once your feet are set, with the front foot slightly ahead of the back foot, and your body correctly balanced over the inside edge of the back foot, rotate your upper body in the direction of travel. The upper body provides the movement in this turn, not the feet.

The upper body rotates inward. It does *not* bend forward at the waist. Your shoulders should be level, not tilted.

It is important in this skill that you rotate the upper half of your body separately from the lower half. To help with this upper body rotation, bring your outside shoulder around to face the direction of travel. Once the skates are set to make the turn and your body is balanced mostly over the back skate, there is no need to manipulate them in any way—no pushing, dragging, or scraping. Your upper body makes the turn, not your feet.

The faster the speed, the less space there is between the skates (fig. 3-11 and 3-12). While the body is mostly balanced on the inside edge of the back skate, both skates should be under the body to provide the most balance. If the skates are too far apart, the body is not properly balanced. Keeping the feet under the body reduces the temptation to lift the toe of the front skate off the ice. In this turn, both blades belong on the ice, not in the air.

Figures 3-11 and 3-12 show the deep edges in this turn and the proper placement of the skates to make a very fast tight turn: both skates are directly under and supporting the body.

3-11

3-12

When you are doing power turns, the inside edge of the back skate does not draw an arc, or half circle, on the ice behind the body. Doing so would cause a scrape on the ice, a loss of balance, and a slowing down. The only noise heard when performing this turn properly is the crunch made by the weight of the body down into the back inside edge.

To help with upper body placement, hold a hockey stick in two hands. Place the middle of the stick on the right hip when turning to the right (with a right outside edge and a left inside edge), and on the left hip when turning to the left (with a left outside edge and a right inside edge.) Make sure your shoulders are level and not tilted.

Stepovers

There are two types of stepovers: one for quickness and one for power. The quick stepovers require agility, and the power stepovers require balance. Both should be mastered. (See chapter one for power step overs.)

When you are learning stepovers for quickness, always keep the skates directly under your body (fig. 3-13). If the skate steps out too wide, you'll lose balance and speed. The body must *always* be supported by both skates in these drills. Both skates must stay directly under the hips.

3-13

When teaching quick stepovers, I ask my students to use the inside edges of both skates: one inside edge to grab the ice and "pull" under the crossover foot, and the other inside edge of the crossover, or landing, skate. For an agility stepover, both skates must always remain directly under the hips. Steps are small and very quick. When you cross right over left, the left inside edge (big toe) will dig into the ice and your body will balance over that edge as the right skate is lifted and crossed over to land next to the left skate on an inside edge. Use the front half of the blades only, not the entire blade. In this drill, no outside edge is used.

Quick feet drills for stepovers:

To begin, step to the side with a right inside edge for the count of one. Bring the left skate to the side of the right skate for a count of two, and step back on the right skate for a count of three. Then step out with the left skate for a count of one, bring the right skate near the left for a count of two, and back to the left skate for a count of three. The weight is transferred from skate to skate for a count of three. The step out should be about one foot to the side. Each step on the count of one should be a small jump. Do this drill as quickly as possible.

Once the above three-step drill is mastered, proceed to the three-step crossover. To do the crossover, step to the side with the first skate on the count of one, cross the other skate over the first skate on the count of two, and step out to the side with the first skate to the side of the crossed-over skate on the count of three. During each count, place the skate on the ice directly under the hips.

Another drill places the stick on ice. Stand, facing the length of the stick and take two steps back and forth, the length of the stick, stepping no further out than the length of the stick. Repeat as rapidly as possible. Repeat the drill using three steps side to side the length of the stick. The more steps, the closer the feet.

Forward Starts

Forward starts can be done with agility, with power, and with explosiveness. The power and explosive starts use the bend/extend technique, with a deep knee bend and a complete extension. The body is always over the pushing skate. It is important that the body is committed to, or directly balanced over, the pushing skate. If it is not, both balance and power are sacrificed.

Quick starts

Place your feet in a *V* position and drop your ankles forward so that the front inside edge is digging into the ice (fig. 3-14 and 3-15). Raise your heels slightly off the ice. Place your entire body weight over one skate and push down into the ice with the inside edge. Keep the *V* position while the other skate lands on the ice in front of the pushing skate in the same position as it left the ice—toe out, heel in. Your body weight will be transferred to the landing skate (front skate).

3-14

3-15

The landing skate blade will now push off the ice, and the back skate will take the ice in front of the skate that just pushed off. The skate will always land on the ice in the same position as it left the ice. Repeat twice with each skate. It is important that each skate land on the ice directly in front of the other skate. This is crucial; if the skates do not line up in a straight line, they will not stay directly under the body, and you will lose both balance and quickness.

You can check the correct blade strike on the ice after takeoff by looking at the mark left on the ice from the pushing skate down into the ice. If the mark looks like a divot and is no longer than two to two and a half inches, you have performed the start correctly. If there is any kind of line on the ice, it means that the skate blade has slipped on the ice. This is a result of not having your weight squarely over the thrusting blade.

The following photos illustrate the quick start. Notice the position of the knees and the skates.

3-16

3-17

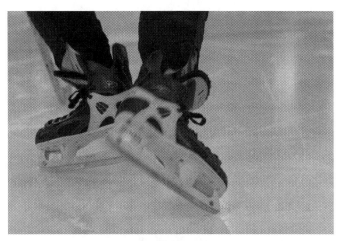

3-18

Drill for agility, or running, starts

Stand with feet in a wide *V,* heels together (figure 3-19). Transfer your

weight to one skate while stepping with the inside toe of that skate.

Only one skate is on the ice. Now, transfer your weight to the other

blade, inside toe. Turn the first skate to an inverted *V* so that the toes

are pointing to the bottom of the *V* (fig. 3-20). Place your weight on the inside toe of the landing skate, and then transfer the weight to the other blade, inside toe, which is pointing inward. The heels of both skates at this point will point outward, forming the inverted *V*.

Do this drill as quickly as possible. Remember, only the inside edge touches the ice, and both skates must be directly under and supporting the body.

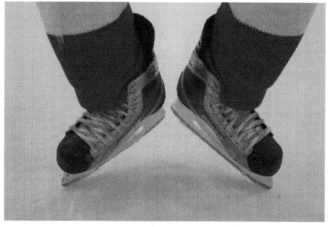

3-19

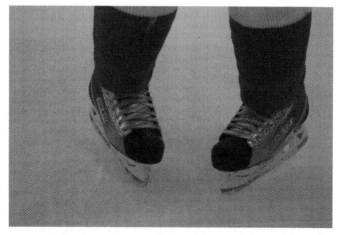

3-20

Variations:

    a.   Take two steps forward with the toes pointed outward and one with toes pointed inward.

    b.   Take three steps forward with the toes pointed outward and one with toes pointed inward.

The above drills can be practiced off the ice. Make a cross with masking tape on the floor, with four even sections. Use the bottom half of the cross to step with toes out, heels in; use the top half of the cross for toes in, heels out.

Power starts

The power start uses the bend/extend technique: a deep knee bend and a complete extension. The weight of the body is always over the pushing skate. This start is exactly like the stride except it is twice as fast with the emphasis on the recovery of the pushing leg. All pushes originate from the knee and not the toe. The skates do not return to directly under the body but to a position outside the hips. This allows for a complete leg extension with the knee lock.

The push in this start is to the side and *not* to the back. Figure Figure 3-21 illustrates the amount of ice covered in the first push. The pattern on the ice is the same as for the stride. The skate blade will not travel in a straight line but at an outward angle.

3-21

Drills for power starts

Begin with two pushes (leg extensions), followed by a two-foot glide. The skates in the glide should be *at least* hip-width apart, never side by side. The knees in the glide will be bent, never straight. Repeat down the ice.

Do the above drill but with four pushes (leg extensions), alternating right, left, right, left. Begin with two pushes (leg extensions), followed by a hockey stop. Face forward with skates at least hip-width apart, not side by side, and repeat the two pushes. Do the above drill but with four pushes (leg extensions) and a hockey stop.

Jumps to practice a forward power start

Begin with your feet in a *V* position and inside edges at a 45-degree angle to the ice. Place all your body weight onto the right skate blade, bend the knee to a 90-degree angle, and push off with the inside edge. The left skate will take the ice in a glide. Stop and repeat the drill using the left foot.

The object is to bend, then extend, the knee in the push forward to get as much power as possible in the leg extension. The deeper the knee bend the more power, because the body lines up over that leg. This drill will help give you the feel of the push off from the ice.

Repeat the drill using the left leg. Once you have a feel for the one-foot push, repeat the drill using a right-leg extension, or push, followed immediately by a left extension, or push. Then extend the start to four extensions, or pushes.

Explosive starts

This start is similar to the power start with two exceptions: the push is not to the side and the feet do not begin in a *V.*

Your left skate will take a position directly under the body. The toe will point at a 90-degree angle to the skating direction or be parallel to the direction of travel (fig. 3-22). Your body weight will be entirely over the pushing skate. The push of the skate will be directly back, not to the side. The landing skate will take the ice with the toe pointed outward as much as possible, and the landing will be on the front third of the

inside edge. It is important that the landing of the skate blade is on a

deep edge. Figure Figure 3-23 shows the correct placement beginning

with a right push.

3-22

3-23

Anything other than a deep edge will cause a glide, and there can be no glide in this start. The landing blade digs into the ice and supports the weight of the body so that the other skate can come forward and land on the ice in the same way. With this start only three steps are needed because each push off will cover about two to three feet of ice going forward.

Side Starts

Place your body weight on the back blade, which will be on an inside edge. The push will be from the inside edge of the back skate to the landing, facing forward, of the same skate (fig. 3-24 and 25). If the start is with the right skate to the back, the push is from the right inside edge to a landing inside edge with the same skate. The toe and knee of the landing skate are pointed outward. The body travels from the pushing skate (back skate) to the landing skate (the same skate, which has gone from an inside edge push to an inside edge land). The other skate, or left leg, is on an outside edge. Its purpose is to support your body as it moves from right leg push to right leg landing.

The movement in this start is like "throwing" the body forward as you push off from the back inside edge of the right skate and land, facing forward, on the inside edge of the same skate. Once the right skate has landed on the ice on a deep inside edge, the next push of that skate is the beginning of the stride. Knees are bent. The pushes originate from the knee, not the foot, and go from a bent to an extended position (bend/extend). Figure Figure 3-24 shows the pushing leg extended after the knee push.

The body follows the pushing foot. In Figure Figure 3-25, the body has begun its turn after the first inside edge push. As the push is completed, the body has begun to turn forward in anticipation of the right inside edge taking the ice in the landing. By the time the skate has landed, the body is facing forward.

3-24

3-25

Jumps for Agility

Start with a deep knee bend followed by a hard thrust of the toes down into the ice. Lift the feet upward toward the body (with bent knees). For better balance, keep the knees in front of the body, not pointing down toward the ice after the toe thrust. The feet tuck under the hips, not behind (fig. 3-26). Kicking the feet backward will throw the body forward and off balance.

3-26

The following jump drills can be performed with both power and agility (see chapter one for power jumps):

- two feet forward

- two feet backward

- one foot forward, left and right

- one foot backward, left and right

In addition, agility jumps can include the following:

- 180-degree jumps forward to backward

- 180-degree jumps backward to forward

- 360-degree jump

Conclusion

This book is not meant to be a compendium of skating skills and drills. It is meant to provide a solid foundation of technique to help you develop into a really good skater. In order to play the game of hockey at a high level, you must first learn and master the technique of skating.

As with all skills, learning to skate takes practice. Developing into a smooth skater takes time and lots of repetition. Practice is the key to developing technique. There is no substitute for practicing a skill correctly. Remember, practice does not make perfect; practice makes permanent.

To help with your practicing, I have produced a **DVD** to illustrate many of the skills presented in this book. The demonstrations in this DVD will help you understand the skating skills and what is needed to make them work for you. The demonstrations will help you achieve a more productive practice session.

The DVD is free. There is, however, a nominal postage and handling fee. Go to www.peerlesspowerskating.com to order your copy.

Gook luck in applying my techniques to your skating. Remember, getting the body involved and feeling what is to be done, rather than going through mechanical motion, is the ideal.

— Eileen Peerless